LIGHT CHASER
A POETRY COLLECTION

CHERYL BABIRAD

Copyright © 2025 by Cheryl Babirad

All rights reserved.

No part of this book may be reproduced in any form or by any electronic or mechanical means, including information storage and retrieval systems, without written permission from the author and publisher, except for the use of brief quotations embodied in critical articles and book reviews.

This is a work of fiction.

ISBN: 979-8-3483-2791-0

Cover images: Depositphotos

Published in the United States of America by Harbor Lane Books, LLC.

www.harborlanebooks.com

I dedicate, "Light Chaser" to those who love and appreciate life, who seek to bring light to their own lives and the lives of others. Through the inevitable ups and downs of our daily lives, it is the seekers and chasers of light who forge onward bringing their positivity, spark and creativity to others.

WHAT REMAINS

Time passes
But memories remain
Family gathered about the table
The conversations
The laughter
Sharing presents beneath the Christmas tree
"Heart and Soul", a piano duet, plays on my mind
Dancing to forever tunes through the night
Warmed by the heating vent after caroling on a cold, winter night
Dinner and hot chocolate warm the night.
Years go by
The people change, the customs too
Classic tunes remain sung by new troubadours
Where there is love, forever love
Memories are made and shared again.

LIFE

Life
Seemingly fleeting, at the moment
It does go on
In spite, of us
In spite, of our worries
In spite, of predictions
In spite, of sorrows
Founded and unfounded
Life goes on
Constantly swirling
Changing circumstances
Changing players
Changing drama
Life's screening
Forever playing.

A DIARY

A diary tells a story
Day by day
Moment to moment
Year after year
Friendships gained
Lessons learned
The joys and laughter
The sadness and tears
The successes, the losses
The family held dear.
A diary tells a story
Of cherished memories
And expectations
Of what is yet to be.

MEMORIES

Where can I go and
Who do I talk to
When life hits hard with
Disappointments, betrayals and such?
I go to my treasure box of memories
Of happier times and places
And think, If I could only take
My happy little people back to
Those happy places with me
With cousins 'round the Christmas tree
With the music and dancing
The light-hearted fun
Child-like fancy and turmoil done.
But life does not work that way
The roses do not come without the thorns
And life is not always like your favorite song
So, I will take my feelings to my journal

Play my favorite song
Face the new day tomorrow
And I will be strong.

PRETEND

Pretend the world
Is as you wish it to be
People are kind
Friends are true
Doors are held
Open for you.

Pretend the world
Is safe and free
That the dreams you pursue
Become reality.

Pretend the world
Is as you wish it to be
And Heaven on Earth
Is as close as can be.

LEARNING

Learning is lifelong
It does not happen in a day
Not a month or a year
Learning continues year after year
There is much inspiration
Through travel and books
People and places
Just listen and look.

A NEW DAY

WAKE UP
A new day is about to begin
WAKE UP
To a new adventure
WAKE UP
To the possibilities that await you
Grab your adventure
Seize it with both hands, held tight
WAKE UP
Make your dreams come true
Only you can do it
Tomorrow is not promised
So, pack your bag
Take your strength,
Your humor, your confidence,
Go forth knowing,
You're the best you can be

Don't let the naysayers put you down or
Turn you away,
Say nay to them and yes to life
WAKE UP!

CLOUDS

Fluffy, white
Cumulus
Sunny days
Darkened predicting
Moisture, rain ahead
Sleepy nights
Stratus
Cirrus somewhere
In-between
Always there
Like the sky
Moving, floating, drifting.

IMAGINATION

Use your imagination
And the world can be your oyster
You can be at the top of the crop
The cream in the coffee
The cherry atop the parfait
Imagination will take you
Places you've never been
To heights you have never climbed
To the stars in the galaxy
If you can dream it
You can achieve it
Let imagination take you there
Pursue your goals
Give them all your strength and fortitude
Do not ever let them go.

NEW BEGINNINGS

Welcome to this new day
A chance to begin again
The slate wiped clean
Yesterday's tears are dried
Errors corrected
We can start anew
Leave regrets behind
Pack your hiking backpack
Put a positive step forward
To the new adventure
That awaits you.

FRIENDS

Friends are not always
Who they seem
Their words are not
Always sincere
But all who enter
For whatever time
Teach lessons
Along the way.

We learn to be discerning
Sorting the positives they possess
From the castaways and regrets.

FAMILIES

Families ground us
At our roots
Support us through
Our lives
They lift us when
We flounder
And brush away our tears.
They give us values,
Share traditions
To guide us along
Life's winding paths.
How wonderful to have them
For support close by our side
To lend that helping hand
When our imminent needs arise.

THE RECEPTION

Where do you go
When friendships
Drift off to sea
When what you planned goes awry
And the new path forward
Is not clear for you to discern?
Do not lose heart
But take focus with
The positives you
Have already gained
And build upon them
Take your steps upward
Upon the ladder to success
In the end,
The reception you receive
The accolades from those who sought
To climb that ladder with you
Will be oh so grand!

SEEMINGLY

I've recently had pause to think
Of school days long gone by
How curious the names heard
Over and over again
The names, you know,
Of the "popular" kids
The chosen ones for all
Once those times are past
And we have all moved on
They are not seen or heard again.

How appropriate that
The shy ones, the quiet ones
The ones seemingly unrecognized
Sparkle, shine and inspire
How true the deepness revealed
Of the still waters
Some never sought to know.

ONE STEP

One step forward
Sometimes
Two steps back
But if we are to succeed
We must stay on track.
You have your dream
Now set that goal
Do not let the challenges
Take their toll.
If you can persist
And keep your strength
Defeat you will resist
And win in the end.

SUCCESS

Success is different
To each person
To a teacher it is
Grateful students
For lessons well taught
To a doctor, nurse or dentist
Healing people's pain
To a firefighter
Saving people's lives
To police officers
Keeping people safe
To a builder
A safely constructed home
For people to live in or
A safely constructed bridge
For people to travel over
To their destinations
Whatever your career or

Profession, occupation
Put your heart and soul
Your dedication and skills into it
Therein lies your success
People are depending on you.

EXCELLENCE

If you use your very best knowledge and skills
Add dedication and perseverance
If you can say you made something
Better than before
You helped others
Along the way
You earned the respect
Of those you have served,
Then, you will have achieved excellence.

REACHING HIGH

Well Done! You did it! Way To Go!
Words we all love to hear
We have done our best
Accomplished our goals
Earned the applause
From family and friends

The steps were never easy
Along the way
But you kept on going
You persevered
You never let ruts in the road
Dissuade you

You held strong
Against any winds
Of naysayers' negativity

You stand tall and proud now
Shouting to the masses,
"Yes, I did it,
I achieved my goal!"

CALM

Calm is the voice
Of the soft breeze
It is the drift
of the ocean breeze
It is the sparkle
Of the stars in the night sky,
The delicate floating
of a leaf from the tree.
Calm is the chirping song
Of the newborn baby birds
As they await their parents return
with food
The bud opening to flower
and greet the morning sun.

ALWAYS HOPE

Always Hope
Keep it in your heart
Have faith
Be confident
To make a new start
Opportunities arise
Select what is right for you
And Always Hope
With hope dreams do come true.

HAPPINESS

You can make your happiness
With calm and positivity
A quiet room
And candle's glow
Relaxing music
Soft, warm blanket
To cozy up in
A good book to read
A favorite movie
Lighthearted and fun
Follow this advice
Your happiness is won.

AGE

Age is not a number
To be counted with dread
It is more an accomplishment
If positively lead.

The friends you've met
Along the way
And more you've yet to meet
The places you've traveled
And continue to go
The goals already met
And dreams to still fulfill
The happiness given
And received
With each age come
Endless new opportunities.

FEELINGS

Feelings run the gamut
Happy, sad
Anxious, mad
Doubtful, confused
With many in-betweens.
There are positives and negatives
Their approaches
We can't always predict
Just handle them
As best we can
Is our sole edict.
The happy, positive ones
We easily go with the flow
The anxious, doubtful and confused
Treat one step at a time
Tread carefully as you go.
You cannot control all things

So do not get mad and pout about
Just keep your cool
It will work itself out.

MOMENTS

Each moment is a memory
To look back upon
Throughout the years.
Each has its significance
Whether it be fondness
And a laugh or smile
Or sadness and regret
Tears, a difficult lesson learned
They are all wrapped up
Together in the life we lead.
Treasure them and understand
Share them as you choose
They will always be
A part of who we are
Never to repeat.

CONNECTION

Connection to home and family
The homeland where you live
Serves to provide grounding
Through difficult times
That may likely lay ahead
We cannot predict the future
But some things remain the same
A home built strong with love and faith
Those who share your joy and tears
A homeland that offers freedom
"From sea to shining sea,"
We are connected to all this
With accepted responsibility
To care for it and appreciate
All that has been given
Just to keep us free.

POSSIBILITIES

So many possibilities
Await us every day
Sunshine to greet the morning
And every sleepyhead
Work to keep us busy, strong and wise
Libraries chocked full of books
Novelty shops and village cafes
Created to stimulate and inspire
Interesting people with whom to chat
And enjoy an intrinsic cup of tea
Bon Appetite!
And as that brilliant sun goes down
As we are about to close our eyes in sleep
Possibilities await in a sky of gleaming,
Sparkling stars
Wishes upon them bring possibilities
Of so many dreams to come true.

TIME

Time is not a friend
Nor those who tell you
"It is not your turn"
"You must wait"
"Yes, your credentials are impressive but…
Good luck, we have chosen someone else"
"Oh, that position has been filled"
Or, "It is no longer being advertised"
Then, there are the turnoffs, the no responses
Ignorance and self-centeredness are never acceptable,
Not in any time, though some may lounge in their naivete,
Their empty promises do not impress
They do not hear
And, time is not a friend.

SUNRISE

Sunrise
And a new day is here
How shall I spend this time?
Maybe a walk in the park
Around the lake
Maybe I will finish that book
Set aside to read again
When I have the time
Maybe I will call the friends
I have not spoken with for a time
Maybe I will attempt
Another story I would like to write
Or play the piano once again
It is up to me
It is my life
And it is "Sunrise."

SUNSET

When sunset comes
I hope to say
I showed someone
A brighter day.

I gave a hand
I lent an ear
For another's loss
I shed a tear.

I did my best
I lived my life
I brought happiness
Where there was strife.

SMILE

A smile is welcoming
It shows you care
And lends brightness
To the day

When shared with others
It lends a spark
Of happiness and promise
For another heart

You can never imagine
The changes it brings
When you add a smile
To everything

DREAMS

Keep your dreams
Let them never stray
Enjoy your life
Find happiness in each day

Choose one moment
One reflection every day
A welcome sunrise
That brings a new start
The magical snowfall
On a winter's morning
Drifting, covering the ground
With its untraveled softness

The long- awaited blooms of spring
The roses, lilies, Rose of Sharon
Pollinated by the bees
Open wide to announce

Their joyful arrival

The warmth of the sun
The forever ocean waves
On a lazy summer beach day
Gathering shells along the shore

The crispness of Autumn
Crimson and golden leaves
Rainbow sunsets
And promises of dreams come true

YOUR NAME

Your name reflects
Your personality, your character
Rose is like a flower
Christie is kind and faithful
Robert successful, victorious
Melody like a song
Berraca is joy
It may be a family name
A tradition
Or one completely new
If you were to select
What name would be for you?

MUSIC

Music is art
A creative muse
A meditation
Of different forms
Whether Classic or Jazz
Country, Broadway,
Rock or Soul
Each of us choose
Our favorite
Music is the heartbeat of life.

CLASSIC

Classic music
Classic cars
Classic tale
Best by far
The new will come,
It too will have its moment
But when the "Test of Time" is posed
It is the Classic
That has returned.

ROSE OF SHARON

Rose Of Sharon
Growing wild
Spreads high and wide
Sharing its purple glory
And a lesson
We need observe.
Unlike poison ivy
Which also spreads, it's true
In life it's better
If you be wise
To spread only the truth.

DANDELIONS

I am strong
And will not be held down
I am on my way
Traveling the less traveled path, even so
I will stay strong
I will keep on rising
I will not be put down or crushed
I have perseverance and fortitude
I know what I want
I have set my goals
My positivity overrides
Any blocks set in front of me.

Yes, I am like the Dandelions,
Those tall and growing Dandelions
Covering the grass you just mowed.
You mowed them down,
But the rain respected them

And helped them up.
They came back because
They were proud, strong, and respected.
They spoke, "You see, world, even we the Dandelions
Have something to show and teach."

LAVENDER

It is summertime
And Lavender Fields
Are calling to me
Do not worry,
The bees will not harm you
They are busy pollinating
The Lavender, beautiful Lavender
The color and scent for soaps,
Perfumes, oils,
Plants for your garden
Bunches for your vases
I love walking through
Lavender Fields
A time of peaceful meditation
I shall go again.

AUTUMN FAIR

Come with me
To the Autumn Fair
There is nothing
Quite as grand
The temperature is cool
For donning a light sweater
And enjoying a pleasant stroll
There are vendors galore
With all handmade crafts
Colorful as they can be
I want to choose everything
There is just so much to see
And then maybe have
A cold drink or cup of cocoa
If you wish
And sit awhile
Beside the lake
Have a conversation

Or just reflect
Upon the day
As new ducklings
Swimming by
With smooth tranquility
Are determined in their path
And hardly notice me

Come with me
To the Autumn Fair
There is nothing
Quite as grand
And sit awhile
Beside the lake
Reflect upon the day

SEASONS

Seasons come and seasons go
Each one has its time we know
But as they pass
We remember still
Next year
Come again they will
Winter, spring, summer, fall
There is something special
With them all
If I had to choose but one
I'd venture it could not be done.

DID YOU GET MY MEMO?

Did you get my memo?
I really do not know
I must have sent it
At least a week ago.
You must be just so busy
And could not find the time
But really, to ignore
My little memo
There is no reason or rhyme.
Maybe the e-mail
Is just too slow
Too many memos left to go
Oh well, this is just little me
Still waiting here
And thought I would let you know.

FOOLS

Silly little people
All about yourselves
Jealous of
The success of others
You hold yourselves back
Don't you see?
Success accumulates
While hurtful vibes
Disintegrate into
Pools of nothingness
Those who are positive
And helpful to others
Go on in spite, of you
Silly little fools.

THESE TIMES

These times, too, will pass I know
And so, I go with the flow
Treading carefully
In my own time
I will keep the faith
And do my best

I cannot change
What goes awry
Only how I react
Stress does not help
Nor anger cure
Only with positivity
Do we endure

History we are told
Does repeat over time

A lesson well learned
Will serve the ages well
Negativity brings the worst
Positivity, no regrets.

RESPECT

Show respect
Not regret
In kindnesses, courtesies
You may show
For little courtesies
Like a "please"
A "thank you"
A phone call
A card
Will friendships
And more good feelings grow
For when, generally,
We ask a question
Apply for a job
It is respectful
It is professional
It is appropriate
To expect

A timely response.
Respect and courtesy
Should never be outdated
Like machines.
People are not machines.

LISTENING

If our desire is
To always learn
Then, listeners
We must be first
We must listen
To what others say
The knowledge they impart.
For everyone has
Their own knowledge
And gifted talents too
The "Companionship of Silence"
Has been tested and is true.
We can learn much more
Through listening
To other people speak
Rather than trying to impress
With our very own feats.

Knowledge is encompassing,
So, use all the senses well
Listen, hear, see, observe
What the world around you
Over time will tell.

EFFORT

This I was always taught
From my childhood days
The effort one puts into tasks
Will in some way,
Come back to reward you.
It may not bring you
The lavish castle or pot of gold you desire
Even the adulation of others
May escape, it is true.

I am happy and content
To have my home
That is safe and warm
Food on the table
Family that is loving
A small group of devoted friends
A chance to spread
Positivity, empathy, and joy

Through my writing and music
Having self-respect,
The sense of accomplishment
Knowing I have done my best
And life, yes life
Is the ultimate reward.

GRACE

Grace brings patience
Faith and hope
In our times of trouble
It helps us to
Slow down and think
To sort through all the rubble
For often times
We think too quick
And then rush to react
Better to practice a little grace
Rather than cause hurt you cannot retract.

THE COMPANIONSHIP OF NATURE

Trees give us cooling breezes
And shade from the heat of the sun.
The ocean too sends its
Cooling breezes and relief
From the heat of summer sands.
The bees pollinate
The beautiful, vibrant flowers
That color our world.
The sky gives us
Sunrises, sunsets, stars, and rainbows
To behold.
Swans, geese, deer
And other nature, show us how
They care for their babies.
We would be wise to heed
The examples within nature
Of love, caring, devotion, and guidance.

Watch the geese in flight
One always goes back to guide,
So that the last are never left behind
What powerful examples
Nature provides us.

POETRY

Poetry has always been with us
In many different forms
Poetry is an expression
Of life, feelings, memories,
Hopes and dreams
It is a meditation
A reflection upon what has been,
What is, what we want for the future
Poetry is different for each person
It is relaxing and healing, thought-provoking.
Poetry can be read anywhere
Sailing on the ocean
Walking through Lavender Fields
Relaxing in your own backyard
Or on the beach
It can be read in winter by a cozy fireplace
Or even at a summer campout

Poetry can be a calm in the storm.
Poetry, try it you may like it
It has been a blessing to me.

THE END OF THE TALE

There never really is
An end to the tale
For there is always
Something left unsaid
Questions unanswered
Mysteries unsolved
What might come next
Around the bend
Maybe new characters
Will enter in
Another fork in the road
More chapters unfold.

CHANCE MEETING

Hello there old friend
What a surprise
To see you here today
After so many years
I do not know
What wave brought
You back again
But you know
I am glad it did
The years have been
Good to you it seems
Your life went
As you wished
You left quite
An impression
A first love in my thoughts
For so many years
You never knew

We were never
Meant to be
But opposites did attract
It was a moment in time
Now only for
The poems I write
I will always wish
The best for you
And I am glad we met
Once more
If we should
Meet again one day
Who knows
When or where
We will smile
And greet each other
Remember
The past together
And go our separate ways
Again.

CONSIDER WELL

Consider well
Before you speak
Your words of choice
Words once spoken
Do not retract
With an apology
Or a dismissing excuse
Like a joke
A kind word or compliment
Will carry through the years
It will bring a smile
And lift the heart
Every time the thought appears
An unkindness spoken
Will carry as well
Its hurt like a dark cloud
Will bring its reminiscence

Of sadness and
A broken heart.

WHAT IS REAL?

Life is real
Not a dream
A rose too
Has its thorns
Some days bring
Happiness and success
Some bring
Troubles and woe
We never know
What each will bring
But what we know
On we must go
And do our very best
Enjoy the good
Yield not to the bad
Be confident and strong
Handle with care
Feelings, yours and others too

For they can dwell
Like lonely, sullen clouds
And explode suddenly
Like an uncontrollable
Raging fire!

PIECES OF A HEART

The daily tearing away
Month by month
Year after year
The stress
The tears
Broken promises
Hurtful words
The family
The friends
Taken too soon
So suddenly
Like a thief in the night
Lonesome
Scatterings of memories
The heart does not break
Overnight
But chipping away

Like wood on a fire
Burning slowly
Leaving pieces of embers
And the scent of memories

LIFE'S PAINTING

Life is a painting
Of varied hues
And brush strokes
We select our choices
Of colors and brushes
From a variety
Presented before us

The colors and brushes
Resemble our feelings
Be they light and airy

Sky Blue
Hot to burning
Afternoon sun
Orange-Yellow to Burnt Orange
Flaming with positivity
Fire Engine Red

Lucky like a shamrock
Bright Kelly-Green
Mystical
Purple like the cool
Night's haze
Soothing like
The Black of Night
Haunting as the
Subdued Tint of Brown
Chilled as the
Icy Cold White snow

The thickness of
A brush and stroke
Exemplify the boldness
Of our actions
In our painting
The fine, thinner brush
Shows attention
To finer details
Within your life
And painting
The delicate
Fanned-out brush
Adds your creative spark

So, it is
With life like a painting
There are times
And situations

That require our boldness
While others
Require more patience
And attention
To the delicate details
Of the feelings
Of ourselves and others

Throughout life
It is the creative spark
That the fanned-out brush
Adds to our paintings
That adds the creativity,
The flourish
To our lives and work

BILLIONS OF STARS IN THE SKY

Billions of stars in the sky
But it really only takes one
One sparkling and glittering
Star up there
To make a wish upon
And make my wish come true.

So please, before I
Close my eyes to sleep and dream
Grant this wish I wish upon you tonight
Keep my family and friends
Safe and warm
And ever close to me
Let peace be among us
For all the rest of the world to see.

LIGHT CHASER

I want to be a Light Chaser
To always seek the good
Be a positive force, not negative
Hold a Liberty torch
To lead the way
Not to light a fire
To destroy the forward path
I want to seek
The lighted way
Not the darkened tunnel
To show the way so others may want
To be Light Chasers too.

ACKNOWLEDGMENTS

I want to thank God for the Gift of Life and the Gifts of Nature all around us. Thank you to my family and friends who inspire and support my writing and everything I have achieved and seek to achieve in life. You are my light chasers! Thank you to the artists and dreamers who inspire with their creativity. Thank you to Harbor Lane Publishing for the opportunity to inspire others.

ABOUT THE AUTHOR

Cheryl Babirad lives on Long Island with her husband, son, daughter and adorable Jack Russell Terrier. Cheryl has always loved reading, writing, playing the piano and teaching. She taught Kindergarten, First and Second grades for thirty-nine years. Now, in her retirement, Cheryl enjoys writing poetry, which she actually began during her high school and college years. She finds writing poetry inspiring because of its timelessness. She says that we all experience many feelings throughout our lives and with poetry we share the joys, sorrows, ambitions and struggles, and offer empathy, encouragement and hope. Through her writing, Cheryl hopes to encourage, uplift and inspire her readers.

facebook.com/AuthorCherylBabirad

ABOUT THE PUBLISHER

Harbor Lane Books, LLC is a US-based independent digital publisher of commercial fiction, non-fiction, and poetry.

Connect with Harbor Lane Books on their website (www.harborlanebooks.com) and social media @harborlanebooks.

- facebook.com/harborlanebooks
- x.com/harborlanebooks
- instagram.com/harborlanebooks
- bsky.app/profile/harborlanebooks.bsky.social
- tiktok.com/@harborlanebooks
- threads.net/harborlanebooks
- youtube.com/harborlanebooks
- pinterest.com/harborlanebooks

MORE POETRY COLLECTIONS
FROM HARBOR LANE BOOKS

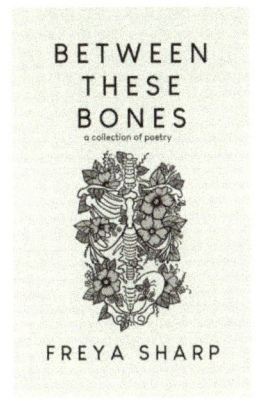

poems

ashes and embers

e. v. nova

BETWEEN
THESE
BONES
a collection of poetry

FREYA SHARP

Evergreen
poems

CHRISTIE LEIGH BABIRAD